My Clean Room

Putting Things in Order

I0901366

Gillian Clifton

SOCIAL AND EMOTIONAL LEARNING FOR THE REAL WORLD™

Rosen Classroom™

I can clean.

My sheets are clean.

My clothes are clean.

My table is clean.

My floor is clean.

My room is clean.

Words to Know

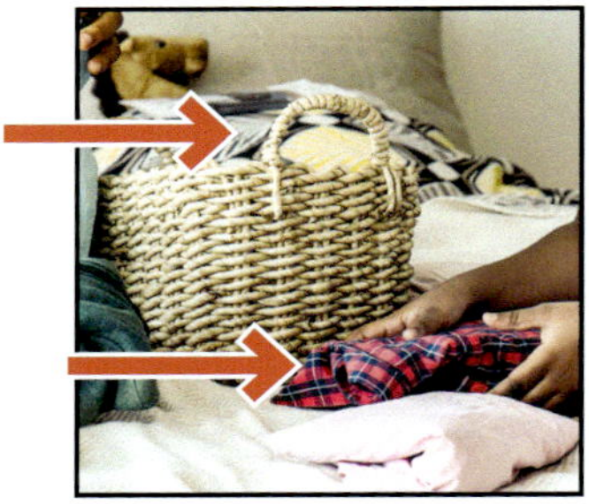

clothes

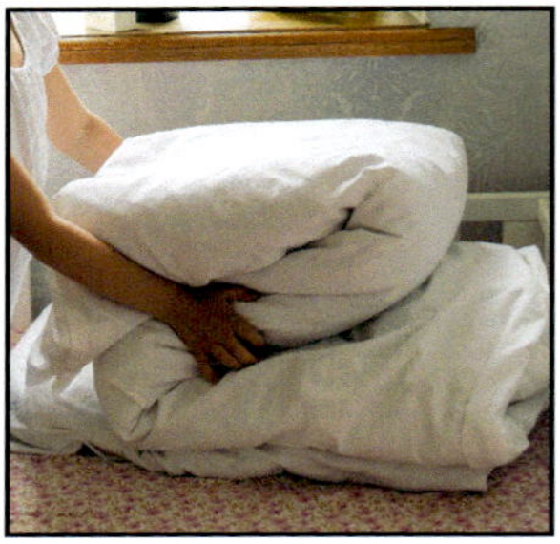

sheets

table